FOOTPRINTS

Walking Through the Passages of Life...

Howard & Jeanne
HENDRICKS

MULTNOMAH PRESS
Portland, Oregon 97266

Design and cover photography by Paul Lewis.
Interior photography by J. E. Edmondson.

FOOTPRINTS
© 1981 by Howard G. and Jeanne W. Hendricks
Published by Multnomah Press
Portland, Oregon 97266

Printed in the United States of America

Second Printing, 1981

Library of Congress Cataloging in Publication Data

Hendricks, Howard G.
   Footprints: walking through the passages of life.

1. Marriage–United States. 2. Life cycle, Human.
I. Hendricks, Jeanne W., joint author. II. Title.
HQ536.H46   306.8   80-25868
ISBN 0-930014-55-3

Table of Contents

Introduction:
Learning from Living

o get the full value of joy, you must have somebody to share it with." Mark Twain said that, and we agree. For thirty-three years we have had each other to divide up grief and to go halves on happiness. Looking back, incidents in our lives make sense and bring satisfaction not only because we have been together, but because they fall into a framework, a design which assumes a symmetry when it is placed in the light of God's plan for us.

East Texas weeds grow waist high. Hiking through them in the hot sun is a parable of our lives. Cool shade is ahead, but to reach it we have to force apart the heavy stalks, skirt the bogs and watch carefully for snakes. Looking back our path is crooked; we're tired and our skin is scratched. We are glad to sit down with a cool drink.

"Did you walk around the lake?" somebody asks.

Did we! Look at the mud on our shoes! Whew! It's hot! Mopping our brows, we describe the rattler we thought we heard. We show the skinned knee where we stumbled over driftwood. We scratch the insect bites and review highlights.

The butterflies lit on the thistle blooms; bees buzzed in the sunshine. A song sparrow trilled in the pine branches. We liked the lacy green ferns tucked away in the thickets. A high-jumping catfish glistened in the lake; we heard the croak of a sullen bullfrog and spotted an upended fluffy rabbit. The leaves rustled and we caught a glimpse of a white-tailed deer. It was great!

Living is what everybody does. We all walk through the weeds. Life, we've been told, is what happens when you're making other plans. Learning from living comes from looking—at everything. The more we see the more we learn.

In the Old Testament primer of proper practice, God's people brought the sacrifice of praise. The praise offering, or *Todah*, was accompanied by a retelling of life experiences where the skill of living was learned. With exuberance the elders reviewed their lives in order that the young generation might also praise Jehovah and know how to live by His holy law.

Living in the late twentieth century is a dangerous occupation. It was no less perilous for God's ancient people; He taught them to give thanks by rehearsing His merciful care. This refreshment by reminiscence is our purpose. If it quiets a fretful heart or soothes an anxious mind, it is worth the effort of our remembering.

Memories, however, come with built-in erasers. "Perspective," warns Henry Kissinger, "will be affected by involvement; the impulse to explain merges with the impulse to defend." We have tried to tell it like it was, with the hope that our readers will move from our recollection to their own experience.

"I am the LORD your God, who teaches you what is best for you, who directs you in the way you should go." (Isaiah 48:17) ◆

From Marbles to Ministry

laying marbles was my favorite boyhood pastime. One day I was busily involved in a game of singles on the sidewalk in front of my house when a man's shadow showed up.

"How would you like to go to Sunday school?"

This stranger had punctured a bad-news subject. Anything with school in it had to be bad. I shook my head.

"Naw!" I grunted.

"Can I play a game with you?" he countered. Squatting beside me, he seemed OK. If he wanted to shoot marbles, I was ready—anything to take on a challenge. We played several games until I lost every marble. (You see, I lost my marbles very early in life!)

After that I didn't care where this tall man wanted me to go; I wanted to follow him. Walt picked up thirteen of us boys in my neighborhood. As I understand it, he wanted a Sunday school class. He inquired of the superintendent and was told there was none available. However, any boys he could pick up on the outside were his.

Penetrating our turf, he ended up with a collection of ragtag, rough-hewn, cruddy kids. We became his fans. I can see us, sitting in a lopsided circle with Walt drawing stick figures to illustrate biblical truth. The primitive stages of audio-visuals!

Often Walt would cross his legs and his giantsize, fourteen-inch shoes would come up in the middle of the group. He never had a discipline problem! We used to think of what one shoe could do if it ever got loose.

Conditioning my heart soil was a godly grandmother with whom I lived. She so incarnated Christ that when Walt presented the gospel, it made sense. It was believable. He dropped in the seed of God's truth and it rooted.

Walt was a bridgebuilder in the people realm. He took us on hikes in the Wissahickon park. He went sliding with us down the snowy 6th Street hills. He took us to the amusement park at Willow Grove and down the Delaware River on the pleasure boat. All of these times were tools in his teaching trade. He never embraced the idea that teaching could be confined to the four walls of the classroom. He was our friend as well as our teacher.

For hours Walt would listen patiently to my problems about school, my girlfriends (none of whom had any idea of my interest!), and my home situation with an alcoholic grandfather. Mostly I dreamed out loud for him my desire to make my life count for something significant. He always seemed to be on my team, not "on my back."

Occasionally, Walt would help me with my arithmetic. Later I learned he had reached only sixth grade in his own schooling, and this fact explained why he would ponder over my problems so that even I would remark, "Walt, I don't know how to do it, but I know that isn't it!"

For Walt, leading me to faith in the Savior was like picking ripe fruit. To me it was no big deal. One Sunday he made the gospel so clear (as he always did) that I capitulated; it all came together. I decided I wanted Jesus Christ to live in me and I told Him that I did. My reputation as a brat began to change gradually, but certainly. Former schoolteachers would come to the witness stand on that. I had a new perspective on everything. In fact, even school changed. Sixth grade was a new—and winning—ball game. Christ was my Savior. My faith was invested in His finished work and my studying started to count for Him.

My memory projector often highlights that circle of thirteen unlikely candidates for God. Eleven of us eventually went into vocational Christian work. In the numerous youth groups I have led since that time, it is always the "bratty kids" for whom I pray and thank the Lord.

I know firsthand that teaching a grubby sidewalk marble shooter paid eternal dividends. ◆

A Kind of Mongrel Christian

ou mean me? God, I thought for a minute You were talking to me. . . . You were? Even though I'm just a little kid? Well, I'm not sure, but here goes."

I stuck my five-year-old hand up in the air. My dirty insides bothered me. Much like rinsing my hands under running water, I wanted to get my heart washed so it would feel clean. A dark something made me do bad things even when I knew I shouldn't.

"God, I know that You are good and I'm not. I would like very much to belong to You and someday to live with You in Heaven." That was the gist of my prayer as I alternately squeezed my eyes closed and peeked at the sawdust floor and the man praying on the platform of the summer tabernacle.

But there was a problem. The preacher didn't say, "I see that hand!" or "Thank you, young lady." Suddenly it was all over and I was in the car riding home.

"Mother, did you know I put my hand up tonight?"

"Did you? Well, that's fine, dear."

In bed I tried to add it up. If mother

didn't think it was important and the man up front didn't see me. . . . Well, obviously God did not think it meant anything either. That was that. Salvation must be for big people.

Six years of grappling with the almost-dead issue brought me to a snowy Sunday night. My gangly legs draped over a living room chair while I listened to a radio evangelist preaching to children. Age did not matter, he said; what other people thought or said was not important. Two people counted: God and me. What did God say? What did I do about it?

Hope sent me flying up the steps, down beside the bed. "Dear God I am so mixed up. But since you are God, You must understand that. So please forgive me if You have already saved me before. I just *have* to be sure. From now on let's have an agreement. I am Yours and You are mine. That's what You said: 'Whoever hears my word and believes him who sent me has eternal life and will not be condemned; he has crossed over from death to life.' " (John 5:24)

I began to tell people in school that I was a Christian. Nobody seemed impressed. So what? Then the day came when a young man acted improperly and I told him to get lost. He called me a square, but I couldn't get away from what God thought. I read the Bible—on and off. I prayed when I was really scared. I decided I was a kind of mongrel Christian, certainly not the pure-bred type like the people at church.

Later this same persistent young man proposed marriage. I refused but he twisted my words.

"Wow! You have just promised me that as soon as you graduate from high school you'll marry me!"

"I did? Oh, NO!" He laughed uproariously. My mind whirled in confusion. I had always been taught: "Your word is your bond!"

Everybody around me smiled. His parents and my parents were best friends. He leaked the word that we would be getting married sometime in the next year or two. I tried to explain to my mother.

"Don't worry. You've got a while to think about it. He's a nice boy."

I was trapped. I felt alone. Nobody would believe me if I tried to tell them that he was not the nice boy that everyone thought. Even if he was I didn't want to marry him.

A family camping vacation brought me to the evening meeting of a summer Bible conference. The speaker was a missionary recently returned from a harrowing experience aboard the hospital ship Zamzam. Torpedoed by a German sub . . . hours in the water . . . hunger . . . fear . . . hopelessness—then amazing rescue and escape.

"It does not matter what your problem is. You cannot lose. You will always be cared for when you place your life 100% in the hands of Jesus Christ. He is absolutely trustworthy. Who will step forward tonight and give himself—or herself—totally and permanently to Christ, no strings attached?"

My Presbyterian background had not prepared me for such outward display, nor would I ordinarily have done such a thing in front of my parents. Only God knew the turmoil in my heart and my complete readiness to direct my life on an upward course. I—and one other person—walked to the front of the large auditorium. A wise gentleman gave me a verse from Philippians: "He which hath begun a good work in you will perform it until the day of Jesus Christ." (Philippians 1:6, KJV)

Returning home I found in myself an incredible boldness. I told the young man I intended to live my life for Christ and probably would never get married. At any rate my plans did not include him. Fear was gone and I began to make plans for training which would put me vocationally into God's service. ◆

Pruning the Family Tree

he phone rang and I greeted a young pastor friend from Arlington, Virginia.

"What are you doing?" he asked.

"Studying," I replied. "Nothing special."

"Are you sitting down?"

"Yes, why?"

"Your father just trusted Christ this evening."

"He what? You've got to be kidding!" I blurted out.

Such an inappropriate response grew out of long detours in our father-son journey. Ever since I received Christ as a boy my concern has been for the salvation of my family and loved ones. On repeated occasions I had broached the subject of the gospel with dad, but his response was less than excited.

My father has always been a very important person to me. Not that I approved of everything he said or did or that I imitated him consciously in any way. We weren't really close friends, either. But he was important in my life because of the indirect impact he made upon me.

Dad was a military man. He had

seen action around the world. During the periods when he was embroiled in battle, I would become very sensitive to his spiritual need. I and my family prayed for him, but at times I'm afraid my faith sputtered. His response was always the same: Son, don't worry about me. I'll work it out with God (as if God could be manipulated like a Pentagon official).

God brought a man into my life, a man with a passion for men. His name was Butch Hardman. One day before we knew each other Butch was boarding a plane in Detroit when a friend handed him a cassette tape.

"Ever hear Hendricks? Here's a tape you should listen to." On that tape I had related my father's spiritual need.

Butch listened and something about the anecdote reminded him of his own father with whom he had shared Christ shortly before he died. He began to pray for this unknown man, George Hendricks. Some months later Butch attended a pastors' conference in Philadelphia where I was the speaker. He shook my hand afterward. That was the only time our paths crossed before a remarkable incident in Arlington.

Butch was driving the church bus down the street, having discharged all his passengers. He saw a man standing on the corner who reminded him uncannily of Howard Hendricks. Could it possibly be . . .? He backed up the bus, stopped, got off, and went over to the man.

"Are you by any chance Howard

Hendricks' father?"

It is easy to imagine the startled response. "Er-ah (I can envision my father's critical once-over with his steely blue eyes) yeah—you a student of my son?"

"No, I'm not, but he sure has helped me. Got time for a cup of coffee?"

That encounter began a friendship, skillfully engineered by the Spirit of God. Butch undoubtedly sensed dad's hesitancy when he discovered he had met a preacher. For a long time Butch did not invite him to attend his church. He simply suggested that dad drop by the office for coffee. Patiently he endured dad's cigar and his endless repertoire of war stories. Before long he also learned that dad had been diagnosed as having a terminal throat cancer.

Months later Butch was at his bedside. "Mr. Hendricks, I'll be leaving shortly for a Holy Land trip. Instead of my listening to you tonight, would you let me tell you a story?"

Butch had earned his hearing and he began simply to relate the interview of Jesus Christ with Nicodemus as recorded by the Apostle John. At the conclusion dad accepted Butch's invitation to receive Jesus Christ as his own personal Savior. Then dad got up out of bed, stood, and saluted with a smile. "Now I'm under a new Commander-in-Chief!" That night Butch called Dallas.

The last time I saw dad alive I could not believe he was the same man I had known. His frame was wasted, but his spirit was more virile than I had ever known.

       In accordance with dad's specific provision in his will, Butch Hardman conducted the crisp military funeral in Arlington cemetery where the gospel of Jesus Christ was presented to the small group of family and military attendants. As the guns saluted their final farewell, I knew God had vindicated forty-two years of prayer. ◆

A Guidance System Unmatched

 oving 35 miles east took four months and a 3500-mile detour. The journey began in a pre-dawn announcement. To me it was off-key; the timing was bad. It did not fit my circumstances, and it did not make sense.

The sun shines hot in late spring in Texas, so southwesterners tend to wake up very early and use the cool mornings for tough jobs. It was one of those days when my sleepless husband started talking long before the sun was up.

"Honey, are you awake? I want to tell you something. I've decided to hand in my resignation."

Sleep evaporated abruptly. I sat up, jolted.

"What are you talking about? You can't just leave. The church is going so well. The people love you—what will they say? And we're settled so nicely, with the new baby and all . . . you can't be serious!"

But he was. "You know how much I love teaching. I just have to get into the classroom. I've been praying a long time about this decision. . . ." He obviously had thought it through and was sure of himself. He was telling more than asking me.

I loved living in Fort Worth, Texas. It was my first real home in the southwest. With the birth of our third child, my heart had taken root in Tarrant County soil. Yet a few short weeks later I would be selling my furniture.

"My goodness! Look at that price! Would you pay that much for that?" People were tramping through my house picking and choosing and criticizing the pieces I had lovingly chosen and lived with. With only skeletal remains, we hitched a trailer to the car and, like nomads, started East. Dad was destined for graduate school; the three young Hendrickses and their mom would spend the summer at grandad's place in the country. We arrived to find him hooking up plumbing. This house was his bargain buy, scheduled for retirement renovation. We would have a washing machine for diapers, but other private facilities were outside.

In the rolling eastern farmland the small fry Texans flourished and counted the days until daddy would be back. He came, and with him news that the seminary needed him right away. Could he come now and finish graduate work later?

"You mean you're going to load it all up and go all the way back to Texas?" Our relatives thought we had come unhinged, heading back to the prairie. Reload we did, sweltering in the August heat, but rejoicing to be "going home." A peace settled over us; our hopes were high.

At a mountain lookout point en route, Howie stopped driving. "It's so beautiful here; let's just stop a minute and I'll check the trailer." When he did, he saw that a crucial nut was lost; the bolt was just about ready to let go. We would never have made it down that steep mountain without a tragic crash. The lookout point turned into the site of an on-the-spot thanksgiving service. Why had we stopped? We were in a hurry; Howie never stopped just to sightsee. The Lord had shown him His stop sign—just as He had shown him the exit sign in Fort Worth.

That dramatic moment of nearly three decades ago—and all of the subsequent guidance system that led to the right house, the right church, the right schools—glows in my memory. "Consider what great things he has done for you." ◆

Moving: A Lesson In Remedial Faith

oving, I suggest, is best for birds. They do it twice a year and have nothing to take with them. The Hendrickses, by contrast, collect junk better than Goodwill Industries—with vestiges of a depression disposition to save every piece of string. Who knows? You may need it some day!

Moving is maniacal. That is my considered judgment as an individual who has rarely moved. One relocation story serves to illustrate my instability on this issue.

A wife, four children, an aging dachshund, and a large German shepherd, together with this Dutchman, were once crammed into a small frame house. It was true that every time we entertained guests, some of the family preferred to visit elsewhere. But every human project demands some sacrifice. I continued to persist, "We do not need a new house—what's wrong with the one we have?"

When unable to convince a stubborn (and prayerful) partner, the best thing to do is to encourage the recalcitrant to do some investigation.

"Check out the possibilities, honey."

I was convinced she would lose heart in the depressing process. On rare occasions I went with her to view some disaster area, pointing out all of the reasons why no one in his right mind would purchase that pile of bricks. I was wearing a smug inside look when a choice personal friend, a realtor, confronted me with the fact that he had unearthed an incredible "buy." It met my checklist of specifications.

Reluctantly I drove to the house convinced that it would be another detour to disappointment. It was a lovely home! The moment I stepped in the house I knew it was what we needed. Undoubtedly, it was beyond our finances; it would require a first-class miracle.

"What do you think?" my friend queried.

"I think it's great, but I can tell it's over my head. How much does he want for it?" The disclosure of the price convinced me.

"Jack, I can't afford that!"

"Well, why don't you make him an offer?"

"My friend, any offer I would make would be ridiculous."

"Well, make him a ridiculous offer." I threw out a figure. Jack blinked.

"Well, that's ridiculous, but I'll tell him. If he accepts, you've got a miracle in the making." That pretty well iced the cake for me and would settle the dust of my decision making. The next day Jack called.

"Hendricks, you have just bought a new home."

"You're kidding!"

"No! He accepted your offer."

"But that's impossible."

"I know. But I once heard a preacher say we've got to trust the God of the impossible—name was Hendricks, I think." Obviously, sloganeering is a lot easier than believing God.

"Tell me what happened."

"Well, I called and said I had a firm offer. He asked how much and I told him. There was a long pause on the other end. I thought he would start swearing at me, but he said, 'I'll take it.' Then there was a long pause on my end as I recovered."

The house was handcrafted for the Hendricks family: well-built and adaptable for entertaining, almost precisely what we had asked God for. It has been our home for a decade. I am convinced that moving was one of those required courses in which I had to enroll for remedial faith.

God is neither a celestial scrooge, nor a sugar daddy deity who overindulges. He can be counted on to provide just what His children need—when they need it. ◆

Dogs I Have Known

A boy in Rochester, New York, wrote the following, entitled, "What My Dog Means To Me."

"My dog means somebody nice and quiet to be with. He does not say 'do' like my mother, or 'don't' like my father, or 'stop' like my big brother. My dog Spot and I just sit together quietly and I like him and he likes me."

When I was a boy, Bliz and I sat together—not always quietly. He was appropriately named, a blanket of pure white, except for two pink ears that stood up like twin peaks. I loved to take my Eskimo for walks in the neighborhood. He was admired by all who saw him, and respected by other canines.

His great contribution to me was his understanding nature. Often when I felt unfairly blamed, I would go out into the yard, tears gushing from my eyes, and tell Bliz. He would wag his tail as if to say, "That's OK, buddy, I understand. Just you and me, man—all the way." Then to climax his commitment he would lick my tears away.

How was I to know he liked salt?

Peanuts (circa the first years of the Hendricks family) was in a class by herself. Honey brown, a soft ball of cocker spaniel, she was beautiful, but not too brainy. She had, however, her own magnetism, especially when in heat. She attracted dogs from all over the county—every size, shape, and description. The fence was high, but, like Superman, her paramours leaped the tallest. And soon—you guessed it—she was in a family way.

Peanuts' major contribution was her provision for our children of superb sex education. As each puppy was born just outside the family room window, she licked it clean and got it functioning and secure. Four children never forgot this feature of their formative years.

Fritz and Boji were two elephantine German shepherds who signed on for guard duty in a succession of eventful years. We somehow attracted dogs who were all heart. Fritz, even after attending obedience school, got his walking papers because he insisted on tearing up the indoor-outdoor carpet on the patio when left alone. Boji, on the other hand, had a sweet tooth for growing things and ate his way right into exile via the dogwood tree and the carefully sculptured boxwood hedge.

Franz was the family favorite. He helped raise four kids, Barb, Bob, Bev, and Bill. Another lower-IQ canine type, he was an affable personality. Invariably he ended up in bed with one of the boys holding his quivering form. Mom, missing the dog, would walk in the room and call, "Franz? Are you in there?" In spite of the heavy-handed jailer, the covers would jump and a shiny black nose would confess.

Occasionally Franz was the reluctant performer in the so-called Newman Clown

Circus—a summer brainchild of the four vacationing B's. He starred as probably the first dachshund in history to be shot out of a garbage can—and live. Indoors he was the hit of the household when he was called from the end of a hallway containing a ninety degree turn. The ell became his waterloo continually as he failed to brake his speed sufficiently on the polished floor to round the corner. Yet his repeated side collisions with the hall table never seemed to dim his ardor for another run.

With a touch of chagrin in retrospect, none of us will ever forget the day Franz disappeared. Mother knew he must be in the house somewhere. She searched every corner, but no dog. Finally, back in the kitchen and utterly mystified, she heard a muffled sound in the direction of the clothes washer. There, peering out through the round pane of the front-loading machine, were the plaintive brown eyes with the black side drapes of ears. For the record, no confession was ever documented in this still-unsolved mystery.

Franz's silky black whiskers turned to soft gray, and he died at the ripe old age of thirteen, greatly beloved. When he became ill on New Year's Eve, no vet was available. We called a family conference and with the aid of our in-house R.N. figured the antibiotic dosage by his weight, and got him going again. But he was *very* tired. On a cold January day when all the young Hendricks brains were in school being honed, a tenderhearted Mama couldn't bear his suffering any longer. She gave him a sedative (left over from the rambunctious days of German shepherd shenanigans) and carried him lovingly to an objective and decisive vet to say goodbye. She cried all the way home.

Funny, pet dogs are not mentioned in the Bible. But they are clearly one of the good things God has given us to enjoy. ◆

New Directions By the Old Rules

fter we watched ROOTS on TV we will never forget the men of the Mandingo tribe dedicating their newborn sons toward the full moon.

When we heard Tevye sing "Tra-dishun" in FIDDLER ON THE ROOF, we looked into a memory mirror; buttons were pushed inside to remind us of the continuity that traditions teach. The way we make a pie crust, or shine our shoes, or celebrate Christmas—a hundred habitual acts—hark back to a former day.

We who predate the Great Depression and World War II saw many traditions altered. When father was out of work, family patterns changed. As a very small girl I see myself piling my dolls into a toy baby buggy as my family prepared to move.

"Why do we have to leave this house, mother? I like it here."

"Well, we just don't have enough money to live here, dear."

"But why can't we get some money?"

"Stop asking questions and just get ready to go."

It would be years before I understood economic downturns and mortgage foreclosures, but my wise father drove the family past our local bank one day where the door was closed and locked with iron bars.

"See that? That's where our money is and we can't get it, so we have to move."

Places, however, do not make traditions. People do. Our new house was not as nice as the old one, but it conformed to a familiar—though less lavish—Christmas. We still had raisin toast and hot cocoa on Sunday evenings. Mother continued to wash clothes on Mondays and to starch her pillow slips stiff. When the wartime economy banned butter, the annual fruitcake was still made, but with oleomargarine.

Two decades after I tearfully packed my dolls, I very joyfully packed another suitcase with bridal lingerie and honeymoon togs to make a much greater leap into the unknown. With a new husband and a married name, I snipped the strings of childhood and moved hundreds of miles to a strange setting. Yet, like Kunta Kinte, our new home bore the stamp of family tradition. From the care of babies to the spending of money we reflected our roots, but not without questions. As Christians we began to ask, Why do we do this—or that? Study of the Scriptures taught us traditions should be tools to teach truths.

Moses taught the Israelites to tie teaching about Jehovah to everyday living.

"When your son asks you, 'What is the meaning of. . .? tell him. . . ." (Deuteronomy 6:20,

21) Why would the son ask? Because the ritual, the symbols, the formalized language over and over aroused his curiosity. Deep meaning can more readily be understood when the child wants to know, when he asks, "Why?"

The made-to-order birthday dinner of fried chicken and mashed potatoes, followed by the annual birthday cake, opened a door for us to say, "Bobby is four years old. This is his special day and we love him very much." Then in our house we also prayed and thanked God for that life and recommitted that child to Him before the candles were blown out.

The formal routine of joining the church at age twelve marked a juncture in life where serious spiritual tasks could be understood and assumed.

Our family vacations were an annual time to inject serious goal-setting for the year amid the fun of away-from-home recreation.

The tradition of a weekend away for mommy and daddy spoke graphically that parents need to be alone sometimes. For us it meant a chance to review our relationship with the Lord and with each other.

Making an annual Christmas tape captured family progress for posterity and said to each family member, "What *you* say is important. We want to listen to you and we want to remember."

Family worship was not a slavish addiction, but a regular practice. It emphasized to all of us what is *really* important in life. Narratives from the Bible were told and retold, and closed with the question, What can we learn from this?

As a family we sang many old hymns and memorized portions of God's Word together. It was fun and it was functional. In later years that base helped us to chew over biblical questions, always being careful to emphasize that the Spirit Himself is the Teacher of truth. Even daddy does not always have the final answers to all questions!

God does not approve ruts; He does sanction tradition. It is a cohesive glue to hold us together, to help provide security in a fragmented world. ◆

Stranger Unaware

generous man will prosper; he who
refreshes others will himself be refreshed."
(Proverbs 11:25)

Among the many reasons God
moved me to Texas, I am convinced,
was to teach me some rudiments of
hospitality. In the Lone Star state,
cordiality is a way of life. I had to learn that it looks
much easier when you are on the receiving end. But,
like all of God's commands, there is a benefit clause.

Could anyone have predicted that
when we invited a missionary from Alaska to dinner
we would hear an evening's worth of spine-chilling
stories about dog teams; or that a missionary doctor
at our dining table would describe to us his
experience of delivering his own child in a remote
area, so that we were all fighting back tears?

Conversely, how much we learned
from the negative comments of a visiting Bible
teacher who criticized our children's prayers. Every
visitor is a new experience, from the genteel
Britisher who offers a free lesson in serving tea, to
the carload of college kids who needed beds on New
Year's Eve when their wheels broke down in Dallas.

What do you do when the blue
norther blows through early and the dinner planned

for forty people in the back yard has to be moved in? You move the cars out of the garage, grab a pile of newspapers and a role of masking tape. In an hour I learned you can "paper" the walls, carpet the floor with old rug pieces from the attic, move the tables inside, and serve a candlelit buffet that the guests thought you had planned for weeks.

Early in our Fort Worth pastorate we invited the entire board of elders and deacons and their wives for an open house. After all, everyone wanted to see the new home which the church had purchased for the pastor, but I had not yet learned the art of asking for assistance. It was my first time to triple my brownie recipe; as an inexperienced cook, I did not make sufficient allowance for the difference in the pans I used—nor did I start early enough to allow for bloopers! Nearly a third of them were burned and there was no time to make more. The pastor's wife violated a local custom—she served store-bought cookies!

During that same era we regularly housed our youth director who traveled from a distance and stayed Saturday nights. I never knew when on Saturday he would arrive; he was a young man who ignored conventions.

A hot Saturday when I was very pregnant, I rested in the cool living room, not quite fully clothed. His jalopy sped into the driveway and he hopped out and flew through the front door without knocking. I recall the panic of hearing his engine stop, dashing for the hallway and tripping on the floor furnace. My bulging front provided a pillow. I was sure I had killed my unborn baby, but

I reached the bedroom when his voice called out, "Hey! Anybody home?" As if I had been there all day, I answered demurely, "Hi! I'll be out in a minute."

One of my most painful and pressurized hostessing headaches concerned a mouse. The ladies' circle meeting would be held Tuesday morning. Hostess: Jeanne Hendricks—new mother, new home owner, newly arrived resident of the community. Ever since the "would you—yes, I'd love to" intersection at church, I had been planning. Menu, childcare, furniture arrangement, table setting, etc. I wanted to impress the Dallas ladies with our new little house out where they used to drive by a cotton patch.

They arrived.

"Oh, I just *love* your pretty house!"

"What a charming place you have!"

"Why, you're a regular little interior decorator!"

Finally, with coffee and goodies served, the circle settled in and the chitchat yielded to last month's minutes, money matters, and finally the "lesson for today."

"Good," I thought. "Everything went pretty well."

Seated where the kitchen was in view, my ear was tuned to the Bible teacher; my eye to the surroundings for which I was responsible. Then I saw—no mistaking—out of the corner of my eye, a mouse; a gray invader of my territory, scampering over my polished kitchen floor at rapid

speed and disappearing into my new kitchen cabinet.
I surveyed the group and decided that no one else
had seen it. What if it came back? What if it
decided to come into this room? Winds of panic
swept over me.

It didn't. The guests left. I found
the mouse's port of entry and closed it permanently.

"A harmless little field mouse!"
laughed husband and sons later.

"Well, he's not welcome here! Not
under any circumstances!"

That night I prayed a new prayer:
Lord, let me be as fastidious in my mental and
spiritual purity as I am with this house. Keep me
alert to any small intrusions that would distract my
heart from serving You. ◆

Three Cylinder Handicap

He was graduated from the finest four-star Christian college. The product of a distinguished evangelical church, he had a good personal grasp of the Scriptures. From a strong Christian family, he was a personable and handsome green shoot—the whole nine yards!

Like many in his league, however, he was riding rather than building on his background. At seminary he was acceptable, certainly not outstanding. He suffered from a severe case of the blahs, turning in papers that would make better kindling than academic projects. He generally frittered away his time.

Toward the end of his four-year tour of divine duty, I had developed an excellent personal relationship and I called him into my office.

"Bill, I'm disappointed in you."

"Really, Prof, why?" His eyes widened and blinked.

"Well, I could be wrong but my evaluation of you is this: you are a ten-cylinder man operating on about three, and comparing yourself with others who have only two."

The atmosphere electrified. He

flushed, stifled internal anger, and left. Apparently he felt he had been misunderstood and our friendship bond weakened.

Upon reflection he cooled to thinking temperature. "Maybe Prof is right. Could it be that he's the only man who loves me enough to tell it like it is? He blew my cover."

In time our rapport was mended. Bill went on to become a military chaplain, serving with distinction and impact. One of the cherished letters in my file is from Bill, thanking me for caring enough to face him with my convictions.

Counsellors can often be cowards, not caring enough to confront. Probably the reason I was sensitive about Bill's problem is that I had walked the same street some years before.

Prior to graduation from Wheaton College, an administrator called me into his office and "read me the riot act." Every time I opened my mouth he told me to keep it shut. I, too, stormed out of his office, hotter than a hornet, only to reflect that he was really right. My conclusion: I finally met the first person in twenty-two years who loves me enough to look me in the eye and challenge me with my greatest problem—an undisciplined tongue. In fact, in review I believe that flaw could have been fatal to my ministry. Another template had been furnished by a Spirit-controlled man who truly loved me, and who, like a good surgeon, was willing to hurt in order to heal.

Too often I have seen marriages go down the drain, relationships deteriorate to the point of destruction, people with glaring personal limitations go unchecked—all because Christians who know precisely what is wrong will not love sufficiently to tackle the problem.

"I was afraid I would hurt their future," is one lame excuse. But that is exactly what happens.

My mind recalls the words of our Lord to Peter when he veered off course; it seems a harsh slash to the disciple who had a short time before confessed him as Lord. "Out of my sight, Satan! You are a stumbling block to me; you do not have in mind the things of God, but the things of men." (Matthew 16:23) These words came from the lips of the One who loves with everlasting love.

A former pastor told me about his experience of sinking into an illicit sexual relationship. He said he felt like an exhausted swimmer battling alone in the pounding surf, unable to escape the strong undertow, about to go down for the last time. On shore he could see all the people of his church. Some were shaking their heads in weeping and despair; others were shouting and shaking their fists in anger and frustration. There were words of encouragement and gestures of good will. There they were, all lined up, watching and waiting for something to happen. Only one man stepped forward and risked everything to plunge into the water and help the victim to safety.

Am I willing to be that man? ◆

Leaving the Driving to Him

"I love humanity; it's people I can't stand!"

I chuckled at the *Peanuts* poster; I would never say such a thing— only I did without knowing it.

"Don't schedule us through New York! I hate New York! I have never met a polite person there—it's dirty! It's crowded! *Please* don't route us through. . . ."

Weeks later I was in an airplane circling the Big Apple on a hot, muggy June afternoon. Our jet from Dallas finally landed—late. Already much too close in our connection to make an overseas flight, we stuffed ourselves into a tardy shuttle bus. I lassoed a slippery pole, hating every jostled moment. Suddenly a divine ruler rapped my knuckles.

"Ma'am?" called a polite young Italian voice in front of me, "Would you care to sit down?" An unkempt teen-ager popped out of his seat and, with a gentlemanly gesture, indicated I should sit.

The bus stopped and started, jerked and churned through the traffic to the proper terminal. We pushed our way through the crowd and raced to the ticket counter, only to find

ourselves at the end of a long seat-selection line. By the time we reached the desk it was almost time for takeoff. The agent looked at our tickets, then back at us, and God gave me a second jolt.

"Say, we're pretty full on this flight," he smiled to my husband. "Why don't I put you two up front." First-class stickers landed on our boarding passes.

During the quiet, comfortable flight across the Atlantic Ocean, the Lord let me in on some secrets. He knew all about how tired we were, how we would appreciate not being in the rear compartment where a high school band was whooping it up. He reminded me that He is a tender Teacher. His tutorials met my exact need—and I very much needed to learn that as He shows me concern, comfort, and dignity, I am to reflect this to others.

". . . the God of all comfort, who comforts us in all our troubles, so that we can comfort those in any trouble with the comfort we ourselves have received from God." (2 Corinthians 1:3,4) ◆

Reading the Wrong Signals

ou know the feeling. I blew it! Not just a tiny twit of a slip-up but a royal goof!

He glared at me. "Honey, we have been married more than twenty years and I cannot believe you did that. Where is your head?"

I met him in Honolulu after three months apart—our longest-ever separation. He was teaching in the South Pacific; I was home in Dallas cultivating a domestic crop of four teen-agers. It was to be our second honeymoon. Now the first evening together I was explaining my reasons for this ill-fated decision.

"Sweetheart, let me explain. . . . She came over and said that her husband was getting ready to take the boys up to the camp, you know, in upper Michigan."

"Yeah, I gotcha! Are you aware that *that* is at least 12 or 1300 miles from Dallas?"

"Yes, I know it's a long way. They had five boys to go; and somehow she knew we had a new, full-sized car, and she asked if her husband could borrow it for that purpose."

His breathing intensified. My speech became more labored.

"And I said, well, I really didn't feel

that I could do that since the car belongs to my husband. Then she turned to the little white car and asked me if that would hold five boys. I said I suppose it would, and she asked to borrow it. I hesitated and thought about how it was the Lord's work, and it was the least I could do. . . ."

"And so you just gave it away, huh?"

"Not exactly. She said while he was gone he would lend us his little VW bug."

He shifted and his eyes seemed to burn holes right through me.

"The worst thing was that the morning I took it over, I drove in their driveway and there was a full-sized Chevy sitting there. I asked, 'Whose car is that?' and she said nonchalantly, 'Oh, that's mine.' I realized that she would not give up her car, and watching them together I knew I was in the middle of a marital argument." The curtain dropped on Act I with no resolution save the firm decision to leave the subject lest it mar our holiday.

Back home we faced a further complication. Our sixteen-year-old son was driving the VW in downtown traffic. Misjudging his distance, he rear-ended another car, breaking the windshield and causing body damage. We proceeded with repairs and thanked God it was not worse.

Soon the little white car came home, very dirty and with drooping tail feathers. Our borrowing friend was tall, muscular, and obviously trying to be witty.

"Sorry about this dragging bumper," he chuckled. "You see, we had to—ah—to—

ah—rent ah—a trailer. . . ." He read my husband's displeasure and laughed self-consciously. I choked with disbelief. Rent a trailer? For that lightweight car—all that distance—in the mountains?

"Ah! This'll be fine, Doc," he quipped as he flexed his immense muscle and bent the bumper part way back in place. "Wash off the mud and it'll be good as new!" He hopped into his polished VW and drove off smiling and thanking us for the repairs.

Our car showed serious problems. An engine overhaul did not remedy the grinding noise in the back; it never ran properly.

What did I learn? My rational husband helped me understand I was not under any obligation to lend the car. When I have serious inner doubt, the best rule is, don't. The guilt on which I acted, I saw in retrospect, had no basis. Because our son stayed in Dallas to work, with our blessing, the leader tried to make me feel we had deserted him— and I felt sorry for him.

It was a primer in decision making. The Lord's words, "Be wise as serpents and harmless as doves," have opened my eyes to the needed balance—to learn to look at alternatives, to talk with difficult people, to be assertive with love.

A by-product of that decision was my harsh resentment for the woman to whom I had fallen prey. I had to examine closely God's principle of forgiveness, recognizing all guilt has been paid by Christ. I could forgive her and forgive myself because of Him. ◆

...And That's Why I Love Her

 quarter of a century with one person! As a second-year theological student I had taken my bride in the humid June heat of Philadelphia. I can still remember how the wax candles melted and I thought I, too, would become a puddle. Twenty-five years later I celebrated in the cool Swiss Alps. Tradition calls it the silver anniversary; for me that is appropriate, for it caused me to reflect on the sterling qualities of Jeanne. What do I appreciate about her? Here is a partial list drawn up during that anniversary summer.

Total acceptance. I was accepted in spite of my sometimes crummy attitude, bull-headedness, immaturity, and lack of spiritual leadership; understood in spite of my being covered over with hang-ups and hold-outs by virtue of past background. Jeanne was a student of Howie—an authority on her partner. It bothered me at times; she read me more accurately than I was willing to study myself. She knew I harbored unfinished personal business. Yet she was not bent out of shape by my idiosyncrasies and my failures. She allowed me to fail and gave me the right and freedom to change. "Love," wrote Shakespeare, "is not love which alters when it alteration finds."

Unconditional love. What do you do with a person who knows everything about you and completely loves you—as is? Not, I will love you *if* . . . but I will love you *no matter what.* Loving when I was clearly unlovely, she seemed to have the Lord as her pattern. She was (and is) not only "in love"; she loves. C. S. Lewis reflected, "Being in love is a good thing, but it is not the best thing. . . . Love . . . is a deep unity, maintained by the will and deliberately strengthened by habit; reinforced by the grace which both partners ask and receive from God . . . On this love the engine of marriage is run; being in love was the explosion that started it."

Spiritual Modeling. It was one of those jagged, ill-fitting days when things do not flow together. Arriving home from my teaching duties at school, I jerked through the evening and night with the incessant crying of a colicky baby. It was a relief to leave the next morning for classes after very little sleep. When I returned the next afternoon, the baby had finally conked out from exhaustion. His limp form lay prone on my wife's lap and on his back was an open New Testament from which a tired mommy was having her devotional time with the Lord. I made a rapid exit to the bedroom, threw myself across the bed and cried, "Oh, God, give me that kind of love for You." Here was a woman who did not have a fraction of what I had biblically by formal training, but who possessed a working agreement with Jesus Christ. It created in me an incredible hunger for the same kind of reality.

Consistency. Like an elevator I move

up and down. I'm hot and cold, in and out, excited and apathetic. My wife seems to be always predictably constant. Though I know it is not without a struggle, she is the best-functioning Calvinist I know. She stubbornly believes God is in control of the world and lives that way. May her tribe increase!

Intelligent support. Even when I occasionally attempt some of my hairbrain fantasies, her support shows. Not that she does not offer constructive criticism; she is no Mildred Milktoast or Dorothy Doormat who never peeps or offers divergent opinion in the name of supposed submission. Even if failure arrives, there is no "I told you so." She is prepared to go to work retrieving, retracing, exploring a better way.

Two and a half decades, more than three now as I am writing this, I see clearly that God Himself brought her to me. "Try it; you'll like her."

I did when I said "I do." Those words propelled me first through a wild auto chase on my wedding night, trying to elude my "friends" and still reach Philadelphia's Bellevue Stratford Hotel (the house of Legionnaire's disease infamy) where we sat up half the night waiting for a serviceman to come and replace a burned-out light bulb! The next day my tired little wife boarded her first airplane for Chicago on which she returned the in-flight meal in a most unladylike fashion!

All those past reveries paraded through my mind as I stared from a hotel window at Lake Lucerne. But enough of my mental diary. Let me give you an assignment.

On your next anniversary, however few or many, strain your brain and ask what do I appreciate most about my partner? What unique contribution has that special one made to me? ◆

Depression:
A Menacing Riptide

hristian workers who man the platforms of evangelical meetings tend to earn hero status. As one of those leaders who has perched unwillingly on a pedestal, I believe we seldom see the struggles that happen behind the scenes—the agony that develops maturity, the difficulties that develop dependence.

People know me as an extrovert, appearing to have things pretty well together—positive, upbeat, jovial, and self-assured.

Depression, however, has plagued me since early in my ministry. Very few people apart from my family were ever aware of this affliction. I shared it with no one and managed to keep it mostly to myself. As public ministry increased, depression became more severe. I could, in fact, detect a clear-cut correlation between the Lord's use of me in speaking and the intensity of the distress to follow.

Frequently I came home from conferences or speaking tours during which God blessed His Word beyond my highest expectations. I sensed the definite conviction that I was ministering beyond myself. But when the plane landed in Dallas, the monster struck. Before long I was drowning:

hope was gone and motivation was shredded.

Unfortunately the spillover splattered my family; the most significant people in my life got the hot end of the poker. Yet they were the ones used more than anyone else to rescue me.

"Honey, you have a right to be tired," my wife commented.

"Don't beat yourself for being weary."

She taught me to accept my humanity, my limitations—the fact that I had a body that functioned like every one else's (including my Savior). I grew tired, as did our Lord when He rested beside the well in Samaria. But, unlike our Lord, I wanted to hide rather than reach out to others.

My wife encouraged me to pray with her and read the Word. I refused.

"I'm not ready for that now," I would tell her.

What would you do with heresy like that (Hendricks's brand)? Her response was to ignore it and keep on accepting me and loving me just like she always did. What did that do to me? It freed me up to change.

Still, it would hit me with the force of a sledgehammer, this weakness called depression. The devil knows this, and he was scoring Hendricks knockouts regularly.

The reason Satan defeats us more than we defeat him is that he knows more about us than we know about him. He is a student of each one of us! If this is true, then what better way to beat me than to jab where I'm vulnerable.

On the other hand, the Word kept reminding me, "Greater is he that is in you, than he that is in the world." (1 John 4:4, KJV) On that basis I finally refused to allow depression a permanent residency. As often as it returns, it is forcefully ejected.

Moving that truth of assured victory from the head to the emotions is a long-term, uphill battle. It is often one step ahead and three down, but the pulling muscles grow stronger as they are used.

How has Christ used this "thorn" in my life?

(1) It makes me a very dependent person. His words burn in my thinking, "Apart from me you can do NOTHING." (John 15:5)

(2) It makes me a more understanding person. If I have this incredibly debilitating struggle, then others also know the discouragement of repeated failure.

(3) It has made me a better-equipped servant of the Lord who can counsel about rebounding from failure. Like Peter, of whom the Lord said, "when you have turned back, strengthen your brothers" (Luke 22:32), I can minister from a base of His strength made perfect in my weakness. (2 Corinthians 12:9)

(4) It has made me a more appreciative child. The Heavenly Father has given me proof of His provision. His power working through my family provided the therapy I needed. ◆

Launching a Son

omeday had arrived. Senior year was sliding into home plate. Other graduations had bloomed and faded, but this batch of sheepskin owners included my son, my fourth and final offering to the grinding gears of the undergraduate brain mill.

Ivy league campuses wear expensive, understated airs. Their tweedish manners, I suspect, are meant to loosen the check-writing joints of alumni—and to relax any parent who may have pawned grandfather's gold watch to eke out the commencement fees.

College towns welcome wide-eyed, well-worn moms and dads with warm enthusiasm. There is hardly time to check into the motel before it's time to go to the concert—or Professor Pettijohn's poetry recital. Tower bells ring. Street corner hawkers peddle the U's special editions. Store windows yammer about special sales of summer reading "musts."

My boy is tired. He smiles; he hugs; he fields the questions with his usual offhanded nonchalance.

"Hope you guys don't mind—I made reservations for dinner tonight."

"No, that's great—where we goin'?"
He names the place with an apology about the price.

"Let's go." His proud father isn't
counting dollars at this moment.

Bed and board behind us, the real
thing emerges with the new day. Seniors have to be
there early. We join other families smiling into their
coffee cups before the trek to the stadium. We all
display the jaunty pride of winners, or at least front
runners who have a good probability of collecting
coupons from wise investments. At the corner traffic
light we pause.

"Boy, wouldn't you know it'd be a
hot day!"

"Typical East Coast in summer—just
be glad it's not pouring rain!"

"Got the tickets, hon?"

Crowds begin to thicken in the
quadrangle crosswalks. They look and sound
surprisingly un-academic.

"Looks like all the shady spots are
taken already."

"How about over there?"

"No—can't you see the sign—it's
reserved."

"Let's just sit right here—you're not
going to see much anyway." Dad's decision fills our
quota of seats; we settle to read the printed agenda.
First, find our son's name, then look over the list of
dignitaries. Reading turns to people-watching—and
listening. Sunshine changes the programs into hand
fans. Grannies wave, baby brothers take pictures,

dozens of kinfolk stand and stare.

"I wish I knew which aisle he'll be marching on."

"Well, you look that way and I'll look this way."

"Hey, here they come!"

The orchestra strikes the march beat; the parade for the parents snakes through lanes of searching eyes. Each of us weighs the significance of the bright velvet faculty hoods and the gait of scholarly unknowns, all being graded for what they have—or have not—done for our personal collegian. Grad students pass in review almost indifferently. They have been here before. Last in line walk the plain black robes of seniors-made-good. They all look alike. . . .

"There he—no—that's not him!" The line advances with stifled squeals, whispers, giggles, and flash bulbs around us.

And then I catch a glimpse, only a momentary movement of *his* step. But he's passed and I watch the back of his head staring forward.

The speeches, the awards, the hooding of the doctoral candidates melt together in the relentless heat. I begin to wish it were over. A note on the program informs us that because of the large number of bachelor degrees to be awarded, they will be delivered at another location.

Applause for the VIP speaker becomes the prelude to a mass push toward the parents' luncheon. Handshakes, back pats, and posing with the diploma will consume the day.

"Well, was it worth it?" The "it" covers years of effort and money, prayers and planning. My husband's question opens the door to a closet spilling with memories and maybes.

I have lived through the process of my little boy bailing out at high altitude. I'm watching his parachute open. I can't predict his landing. Whatever I've had to do with it is behind me. It's all in his hands now—his and His—the God who gave me that last little infant and Who cares more than I do what happens to him.

A shiver chills me. At the same time I am tense with anticipation. "Lord, he's yours. We agreed twenty-two years ago. Please take good care of him. But then, You always have. He's my young Joshua setting out to conquer the land: 'Be strong and courageous. Do not be terrified; do not be discouraged, for the LORD your God will be with you wherever you go.'" (Joshua 1:9) ◆

Diploma For a Dad

**B**oston in the June sun. Humidity high and breezes out of stock. Yet the air was alive with the festivity of another college finale. Shaded by an ancient elm tree, I moved only my mind and my eyes to frame the scene for my memory file.

Alumni, packaged in class groups, strode past the rows of seats stuffed with clapping, cheering friends and relatives. The sole survivor of the class of '02 led the parade and proved to be the leading crowd pleaser—a hero for lasting this long! Important personages were conspicuous by their presence. Names like Kennedy, Schlessinger, and Richardson led a procession larded with VIP's.

My seminary professor's paintbrush broadstroked a background of many such ceremonies. How often had I walked the aisle, robed in academia, reflecting on final grades and future destinies in my control? Now I sat watching one that was radically different—not just another commencement, but the culmination of what to me was once an absurdity.

I saw again that first little apartment with the bare wood floor.

"Mr. Hendricks, I can sell you the

perfect policy. You really need to think about his future education. It'll pay off when it's time for college."

"No, I'm sorry. Can't do it now. Not on my salary."

Why had I apologized? This insurance salesman could not understand the principle of eternal dividends. My teacher's salary barely provided living money, let alone establish an endowment for higher education. Jeanne and I talked often—and reminded God more frequently—that the kids were growing and. . . .

"Honey, we're just going to have to trust the Lord." Privately I wondered: Is this faith or foolishness? I was tempted to laugh like Sarah behind the tent door. God had promised Abraham a son through Sarah, but they were too old; it was illogical. God had promised to supply all of my need, but college tuitions being what they are, . . . Lord, I thought secretly, You have got to be kidding!

Speeches—the slave price paid for attendance—exuded idealism. Students clapped vigorously; adults politely patted their palms. Humorist Art Buchwald interlaced his address with one liners of choice wisdom. New Englander Patrick Moynihan challenged America's future brain trust to be the best ever. In the black-robed audience sat my son, my *omega*,—last of the Mohicans. Three had already passed this way.

By all standards of rationality, the reservoir of resources should have been drained by now. Yet, like the Old Testament widow's cruse of oil, the Hendrickses' bank account met each semester's cover charge. I was sitting here as proof of His divine endowment. "Seek first his kingdom and his righteousness, and all these things. . . ."

The moment of truth—the presentation of diplomas—applauded platoons of gowned graduates. In the mass production I did not even get to see the MIG (most important grad), but there was no need to see.

With bold relief I glimpsed the glory of another of the Master's marvels. I did not do this; my son was not here on his own; this whole spectacle is impossible. And I remembered: "Impossible" is the Lord's specialty. ◆

A Purplish Pain-in-the-Neck

other-in-law lists on the family playbill in small print. Joke books color her a purplish pain-in-the-neck. Husbands often harbor a private vendetta against her, and young wives wistfully wonder with their girlfriends how to revoke her family membership.

Nature has ordained that mothers are losers—eventually. The new green shoots must overtake and supplant the older ones. It is a fact of life, simply a piece of the family scrapbook—until you become one. Then the term "mother-in-law" sheds its shell.

The molting season creeps up softly. Daughters-in-law begin usually when you do not even know it. One of mine started in a hotel room where I chatted with my son's new youth co-worker. The other was a nameless face in a college seminar. She smiled at the door and said, "I've wanted to meet you; I dated your son. . . ."

"Well, Mom, what did you think of her?"

"You mean just as a girl, or as a future wife?"

"Oh, Mom! I mean just as a friend."

But he does not ask that question about "just a friend."

What matters, of course, is not so much what I think of her, as what *he* thinks of her. More importantly, what does he think of me? It's scary—my sons' wives are their translation of my womanhood.

I have tried to pull apart the knot that ties a mother's heart into spasm when her son marries. Somewhere between the glory of "she has borne a son" and "he has taken a wife" I must expand. The transformation of little boys into men is one of the wonders of nature. He's tying his shoes, then tying his tie; the next day, it seems, he is tying the knot of matrimony. On the face of it he appears to have discarded good old mom for a lovely young bride. Has he really outgrown his need for a mother?

My heart says no. My mind says, well, possibly. I learn they are both right. If I choose to believe that he is deserting me I will become bitter and competitive against that one whose love drew away my home-grown specimen of manhood. The critical question, I must remember, is not who is she; rather, who am I? What pattern prompts my son to reach out for his own choice, to act out his own version of man and wife? He has, in fact, affirmed me.

My fears that this young beauty will never be able to take care of my boy as I did are probably true. But then his father survived. Can I ever erase that scene I flubbed when his grandmother handed me a pile of darned socks?

"Now, my dear, these are all ready

to wear. Keep them up-to-date. You can start off
with everything mended."

"Oh, yes I will. Thank you." Me?
Darn socks? I never thought about that. I suspect
she saw my clumsy fingers. In her presence I had
once fumbled through sewing on a button.

Little girls, on the other hand, tend
to light the wedding candles long before the groom
shows up.

"I'm going to marry daddy when I
grow up!" That's kindergarten talk. In junior high
she stares into the mirror and sighs, "Mommy, do
you think *anybody* will ever marry me?" Her high
school diploma is brand new when she bursts in
with, "Guess what, mother? He introduced me to his
parents—do you think he's serious?"

We answer five false alarms before
the real fire starts to burn. By the time the wedding
bells ring he has already raked our leaves, fixed our
flush tank, and borrowed my husband's best tie.
How did we ever live without him?

Mother-in-law means a new act on
stage. I am more spectator than participant, an
applauding fan more than a critical coach. Rehearsals
are past and the curtain has risen on the revised
version. My part is behind the scenes—praying,
encouraging, assuring these new marriage partners
that they are winners because I know—by God's
grace—what went into the production. ◆

Father Fever
On The Bride's Day

arly in the day the bride's father fever subtly set in. A slight tremor while shaving, a vague uneasiness when my wife jokingly welcomed the morning with, "Hi! This is the day you sign on one more insurance beneficiary." No reason to panic, but why do I suddenly want to join the French Foreign Legion?

I tried to assure myself: this is no big deal. Weeks of planning and parties, piles of gifts and good wishes all belong chiefly to the women of the family. The clergy is called for the knot-tying, and it should be a very simple matter to perform Bev's wedding. How was I to know that marrying your own daughter is in a different league? Liturgical textbooks avoid such reality orientation.

Our daughter's choice of a Christian young man of integrity and commitment was a delight to us as parents. He had clear-cut goals and intense personal love for our much-loved third child. What could go wrong?

The rehearsal of the ceremony and dinner to follow introduced the gala occasion with no hint of any snafu. Next morning the tuxedos from the rental company arrived without those buttons which hold the outfits together and one of the groomsmen was left without dark shoes. The groom was temporarily missing his pants, and one usher completed his duties with sleeves down to his knuckles. Such minor features are par for the wedding day course. And if one is willing to miss the wedding brunch they can be righted.

We even arrived at the church on time. Everything was on schedule. Mothers were ushered in and soon my daughter and I were to make our grand entrance.

Suddenly the blood was draining out of my system. Some say I looked like I had come from a coffin; color photos confirm this rumor.

"Smile!" called the roving camera crew. I tried and it was a mistake, resembling a bad makeup job on a sad clown. No time to readjust; the organ was playing our song.

The groom's uncle did a magnificent job with his first part of the service. At the point where I would make my first vocal contribution he asked the expected question, "Who giveth this woman to be married to this man?"

For one accustomed to public speaking, there should be no difficulty with this one-liner. My mind, however, went as blank as those of some of my students at exam time. I do not think I could have given my name, so incapacitated was I at that moment. The pause turned into a slice of eternity and eyebrows began to rise in my direction. Inside my head a desperate argument was taking place. "Say something, stupid! What's your line?"

"It's-ah-ah, 'her mother does—and I
do, too'—no that's not it!"

"Well, say *something....*"

Finally I blurted out, "I *do!*" I
sounded like a collapsing groom. A ripple of laughter
spread through the audience, as they all learned I
was very human. No real reason to doubt it anyway.

At that point I stepped forward to
continue my part in the ceremony. Already rattled, I
was in no way prepared for the tender vows which
this devoted bride and groom were to recite to each
other from memory. I have been in a number of
sensitive situations, but never had I encountered the
passion of this one. My eyes filled with tears as I
watched two young people recite meaningful
promises with deep conviction and personal
commitment. Through my tears I watched an
audience join me in emotional involvement. Had we
struck a match, it seemed we would head for the
moon. The rest of the service settled gently to a
beautiful finish. (My bias!)

My conclusion is that weddings can
be routine and often are, but not when the one
being married is *your* daughter with whom you have
the choicest of personal relationships. Suddenly the
fatherly affection of a lifetime focuses in one burning
moment. In an age of throw-away marriages it is
refreshing to feel the weight of this experience
where a couple forges themselves into an all-
consuming life partnership.

Study overseas carried the
newlyweds out of my sight for a full year. The fever
subsided and I discovered that God had chiseled out
a space in my heart just the right size for a new son. ◆

Job Opening in a Growing Corporation

EXCLUSIVE OFFER!

 position has just opened up in our firm for two bright, talented, responsible individuals who are interested in permanent placement with a growing, expanding corporation. The couple must be young at heart and preferably have a strong background in child rearing, with specialties in walking fussy infants and short-term babysitting. Patience and a positive attitude are essential. A good memory for remembering birthdays and ages is desirable. The hours are flexible with some night work and weekends, but we guarantee job satisfaction. Payment is in the form of jelly kisses and tiny hugs; fringe benefits are plentiful. On-the-job training is offered. Position must be filled by May . . .

Are you ready for a change in your life? Then this opportunity is for *you!* If qualified and enthusiastic, please contact our firm immediately as this offer may not happen twice in a lifetime.

That is how grandmotherhood began. The mailman brought it. It is a delicate overlay of sweet innocence to refresh an often curdled complex of living. The attached note explained it all.

Dear Mom and Dad: . . . my doctor says I am perfectly normal, and that if I can live through these first months, I may even *enjoy* being pregnant . . . I can't stand to cook . . . I really do try to ignore the symptoms . . . nothing worse than sitting in a meeting wondering if your dinner will stay put for an hour or so. . . .

A delightful, expectant period of waiting began with that letter. Waiting for the word to come.

Other telephones ring the same, but *my* phone dings with inflections. That day it rang with a smile. I "knew" it was the Kansas hotline. "Mom! It's a girl."

Hours later I set my suitcase down in the apartment which had been carefully groomed to pass mother's muster. The immaculate nursery shone with sunny yellow accents, a rainbow arching over the waiting crib. Next stop, hospital nursery.

A soft, gray-haired nurse pushed the special crib with the pink-blanketed baby to the viewing window. I sang a silent doxology. This was Alison. She moved her tiny mouth and extended a petite finger. For an instant she lifted her little head, and the logic of my heart ranked this wee newcomer as extraordinary. The new mother, even on her wedding day, had not looked more radiant.

Strains of a counter melody in a minor key intruded. There in the sunshine of our family joy, as if in the shadows, was a lovely, red-haired roommate who had given birth to a handsome baby boy. Yet her demeanor was somehow sad, her visiting family strangely quiet. Her young husband, the sullen man in the leather jacket, came briefly and sat smoking silently, as if doing time behind bars. I learned later that he deserted his home in a few short weeks.

During my final hospital visit I waited in a room where a very young gentleman of about eight years, bright and articulate, told me that he was waiting for his aunt who was visiting his dying mother. He had no father and his aunt had informed him that she was "looking for a place" for him to live.

God's reminders strike deeply. I told the little boy about the Heavenly Father who loved him, and I prayed silently that he would come to know the eternal care of our Lord. I felt almost guilty over being so ecstatically happy because of my new gift, this exquisite child born to a loving couple dedicated to being the best parents possible.

The great going-home day came. It was decided that grandmother should carry Alison. What a high honor! I would actually transport this precious cargo up the steps and over the threshold. I would introduce her to the cheerful nursery.

So engrossed was I in devotion to my task, I did not notice a strange odor about the mint green layette clothing. But, as I began to deposit my darling little granddaughter in her crib, I noticed—she was altogether human. She had greeted granny with messing her pants—and dress—and blanket. She would be laid, not under the rainbow amid the stuffed toys of the cradle, but on the changing table to be washed and changed and introduced to baby care such as it really is in mundane day-to-day reality.

Grandparents usually think about what they will teach their young come-latelies. But I have already learned much myself from Alison. Have I forgotten—or did I ever really know—how very demanding is the new life? Maria Montessori, famed Italian physician and child analyst, said, "The one thing life can never do is stand still." Food and loving care are constantly critical for the newborn. She sleeps, totally dependent, completely vulnerable.

I transfer the scene to the spiritual life. Nourishment from the Word of God, comfort and protection for my defenseless soul from the Holy Spirit. "I will not leave you as orphans; . . . (John 14:18) "Like newborn babies, crave pure spiritual milk, so that by it you may grow up." (I Peter 2:2) ◆

When Minor Surgery Turns Major

For most people, hospitals are fine if you need them, but to be avoided like the black hole. Not for me. I am a frustrated surgeon. A favorite pastime is watching the scalpel in action. Nothing fascinates me like the human body.

The day I took Jeanne in for an operation, however, the hospital had grown horns. A doctor friend of repute says, "Minor surgery is the kind other people have; major surgery is mine—and my loved ones." By any standard we were looking at giant-size surgery.

On the day of admission the whole institution began revolving around my woman. In her room technicians came with tubes and smiles and left with blood samples. Prim nurses and hobbling patients passed the door and we tried to talk naturally, but it came out falsetto. Finally I kissed her goodnight and drove home to a cold, empty bed.

Next morning I stood like a parade spectator as the orderly wheeled her down the hall. Her strong reaction to even minimal drugs was evident. She was pale and listless when I kissed her goodbye. It all seemed so final.

Then the interminable wait began. I
reviewed promises from the Word. I talked
spasmodically with other visitors in the waiting
room. A choice friend dropped by and seemed like a
visiting angel. My heavy reading yielded to inane
magazines, which soon gave way to sky telegrams. I
needed to remind Him again of *who* was being
operated on. It was twenty hours crammed into two.
Then the nurse came and said I could see her. But
how? Dead or alive?

She never looked more beautiful,
although frankly she resembled a candidate for the
local mortuary. I bent close and whispered, "Jeannie,
I love you." Never had I meant it quite so deeply.
She mumbled. "It's all over sweetheart," I said. She
nodded and slept.

Recovery was rapid; I was her
personal therapist. When the doctor said, "Now try
to walk a little," I took him literally and forced her
out of bed onto her feet. She would walk if it killed
her.

"Honey, I can't . . . not so fast . . .
oh, honey, this is too much!"

"C'mon, you can do it . . . you'll
make it . . . forget the pain, just keep going. . . ."

Go she did. Her color and spirits
rose almost hourly.

"You know, you'd almost think you
wanted to get out of here early," joshed the doctor.
"I think you're going to break some kind of record.
You want to leave tomorrow?"

The next night my bed was warm
again. I kept reaching to assure myself she was really

78

there.

Lest I forget, the mailman brought me souvenirs of the surgery: hospital statements, doctors' bills, insurance forms. Lest I remember the wrong things, God brought me follow-up thoughts: deep praise to Him for my lifetime partner, profound gratitude for good medical help, and new appreciation for the faithful Shepherd who tenderly cares for us. ◆

Warning! This Calamity May Not Be Fatal

Timing is part of teaching. Hard lessons always appear to be ill-timed. There is never a convenient season for the robber to break in, for money to run out, for a loved one to die.

Without a cue, cancer staggered onto the stage of my young adulthood. The disease elbowed its way into our family, crushing my dad in a dismal, dead-end defeat after eight months of valiant personal combat.

Twenty years later I was traveling in the Holy Land when the fear stabbed me like some ghost from the past. In rural northern Galilee we were housed in a kibbutz at the end of a hot, dusty sightseeing day. Welcoming the immaculate bathtub filled with clean water, I luxuriated, pampering my tired self . . . when suddenly out of my deepest recesses the old enemy called to me—I felt a lump! I tried to deny it, to explain it away, but it would not be ignored.

Mentally I grabbed myself: "Just calm down! Don't jump to conclusions!" With fierce inner determination I decided to reserve judgment until tomorrow. I dressed and said nothing; I could not ruin the whole trip. Tomorrow, and tomorrow, and tomorrow came and went; the lump remained. Ahead lay four weeks of travel in Africa; I *must* tell my husband. Jerusalem, I concluded, was the place to detonate my private bombshell.

Morning came very early because I was only flirting with sleep. I turned to check the time and my movement brought a cheery good morning from my husband. This was it.

"Honey?" My voice quivered.

"What's the matter?"

"I-I-have to tell you something. I've put it off because I didn't want to spoil the trip, but I have a lump in my breast. . . ."

Within hours we had an appointment with a highly qualified physician connected with the famed Haddassah hospital. Ever since I heard about the chapel windows designed by Marc Chagall, I had wanted to see them. But this day we had only one objective: find the doctor whose name was scribbled on our piece of paper.

Everything and everybody was Hebrew. My husband's knowledge of the ancient language helped very little. We found an automatic elevator, but the buttons might as well have been imprinted with Sanskrit. Trial and error taught us that there were three sub-basements in the huge medical complex. People moved in and out always in a hurry. Over and over we asked, "Do you speak English?" One kind gentleman in a white professional coat, gave us directions. Corridors were crowded with patients; noise and hubbub contrasted greatly with the quiet, polished halls of most American hospitals.

Finally we found the door with the right name. In the hall amid litters with patients in all kinds of conditions, I sat on the one vacant chair for an interminable ten minutes. Then the physician with a heavy German accent indicated that I should come into his office; my husband was to sit in the chair. With little fanfare the busy professor of surgery explained to me that at least 85% of these types of lumps are cysts which can be easily aspirated. Judging from my history, he was sure this was my case. Staring at his ceiling, I lay stiffly on his examination table.

"You veel feel only a leetle preeck auf the needle," he said as he applied a topical anesthetic and inserted the syringe. As he withdrew yellowish fluid, he smiled. "I vas lucky; I heet the right spot!" Then he called in my husband and summarized for him.

Six weeks later I sat in the office of my American internist who grinned at my anxiety-ridden story. In his Texas drawl he said, "Mrs. Hendricks, may I tell you that the country of Israel is far and away the foremost in the world when it comes to breast cancer. They see more of it than anybody else and their research is way ahead of the rest of us. You could not have had your problem in a better spot on this globe!" He assured me he had received a follow-up report and the lump was benign and probably non-recurrent.

Again my Heavenly Father confirmed to me His wise words: "Trust in the LORD . . . . He will make your paths straight." (Proverbs 3:5-6) ◆

"Not Every Life Turns Sour"

How many men do you know over the age of fifty-five who are still tracking for God? That question was hurled at me rather pointedly; upon reflection I admitted, "Not many."

But why? Why are many middle-aged people, men *and* women, sliding for home? Reaching for the bench? At the time when they should be tackling the greatest challenges, they are counting the days to retirement—retirement being defined as "doing nothing."

Removal from the mainstream has never appealed to me as a live option. To be sure, I know leave-taking is in my future. Each paycheck deduction reminds me that I am squirreling away nuts for winter, but I have made an unsettling observation over the years: the average time between retirement and death is often very short. This brief postlude seems to be related to loss of purpose, to lack of a sense of meaning and of contribution. Yes, the veteran needs to change his pace—or his place—of investment, but not his objective. Perhaps he needs to do his work differently, but do it he must.

Visiting Palestine, Jeanne and I toured the Nof Ginosar Kibbutz in the Galilee. We were escorted by a bright-eyed host who emigrated from a European Jewish ghetto nearly a generation earlier. He took us to a small electronics shop staffed with elderly citizens. There, he explained, everyone made a contribution. Age was no hindrance. If a person could work only two or three hours per day, he was paid accordingly. But he must work. Each was absolutely essential as a contributing member of the community.

That's it, I thought. An asset, not a liability—a giver, not a receiver in the group. Relaxed giving should describe our most mature years. We need to take a page from the life of our oriental friends who venerate old age. Youth-oriented societies focus on production and tend to downgrade discernment when they put older people out to pasture.

Pedestals in our day are empty. Role models are scarcer than Edsels. Paul wrote to Titus that older men and women have teaching responsibilities. They need to demonstrate to the younger generation a living pattern of prudence and perception out of the most enriched period of life. Their impact comes from a permanent residue of wisdom.

Cicero wrote brilliantly on this topic.

> "But, it will be said, old men are fretful, fidgety, ill-tempered, and disagreeable. If you come to them, they are also avaricious. But these are faults of character, not of the time of life . . . they think themselves neglected, looked down upon, mocked . . . yet all these faults are softened both by good character and good education. . . .

84

The fact is that, just as it is not every wine, so it is not every life, that turns sour from keeping."

Maturity makes its greatest contribution in dispensing courage. The very presence of gray-headed dignity says, "Hang on." Moses urged, "Be careful . . . do not forget . . . teach them to your children and to their children after them." (Deuteronomy 4:9) The torch to be passed is the concept of God's character. Isaiah wrote it in these words, ". . . fathers tell their children about your faithfulness." (38:19)

By any standard King Hezekiah was a successful and effective leader. Yet when in later life he was faced with the end result of a poor decision, he said selfishly, "There will be peace and security in my lifetime." (Isaiah 39:8) An ancient existentialist! No concern for the future generation. Little wonder that his son, Manasseh—born in these late years—became the worst king Israel ever had.

In contrast, many have filled their final years with life. A Navy commander moved abroad to run the administration for a missionary enterprise. An accountant became a specialist for financial planning of God's work. An older widow is personally fulfilled as she serves as secretary for a mission headquarters.

When the secular workaday world puts our personnel folder on microfilm and offers a farewell gold pin, it can be, and often is, merely the overture to a rousing new performance. ◆

And Then There Were Two—Again

few years ago we presented to the adult world our last child—he flew the coop and I've been humming hallelujah ever since.

Jeanne does not join me, at least not very loudly. Not that she's not delighted with her completion of the parental role—who said we are ever really through? But her perspective is different. Let me share mine.

Nothing was more fulfilling nor frustrating than being a parent. When finally qualified, I was out of a job. Like anything with purpose there comes a time when you are finished; for better or worse you have done what you started out to do. In weaker moments you wish you could do it over, but only if you had your present quota of wisdom and insight. This is not a choice.

I have often wished that God could give us one set of practice children, then the second set for keeps. Perhaps our hang-up is in thinking we could ever do it right, even if we had 100 chances. Part of being human is our severe limitations, especially in light of the Fall's blast. Finiteness involves failure. There are no perfect parents. Ultimately the test is not only what we do but what our children do with what we have done—failures and all. We must open the door for them to try.

One of the primary tasks of parenthood is to prepare children to leave. Notice that the command was given to Adam and Eve: "For this reason a man will *leave* his father and mother and be united to his wife, and they will become one flesh." (Genesis 2:24) This statement was made by the Lord God in Eden before they disobeyed and before they bore children.

Often the last thing to be broken is the psychological umbilical cord. Christian parents are often guilty of emotional incest. They lock a vise grip on their children and in the process cripple their young marriage. In our culture we have approximately eighteen years in which to pull this off. Then why deplore what you were seeking to develop?

Psalm 127:5: "Blessed is the man whose quiver is full of them (children). They will not be put to shame when they contend with their enemies in the gate." A searching test for parenthood—can our children function in the market place, in the real world—away from us and our direct influences—not under our thumb?

One day you wake up the way you started—all alone with your partner. The question now is, what kind of a relationship have you built? Is he or she your greatest friend? Have you crafted the components of companionship? What do you have in common that your children do not furnish?

Approximately one-half of marriage is spent without children. With all my faults, wife strife is missing; Jeanne and I enjoy a smooth blend of bride and groom-ism. No one begins to compare with her friendship, her conversation, her sharing of my life.

God still has much for us to do with our married children. I am still learning to plow that field. As I do, I gain expertise with the children of other people, some of whom did little better than we as parents. Perhaps we can help others' children just as others have greatly and significantly contributed to ours.

Ministry is to be equated with life, not just some period in life. When one set of tasks is completed there are others awaiting our time and energy. I would not trade anything for parental privilege.

Having made our impact on this realm we must move on to additional responsibilities. The great contribution now to our children is prayer, personal support, modeling, affirmation, counsel when it is sought. Life and ministry do not begin at forty; they do not end at sixty-five. ◆

Finishing Touches

etting ready for death is not morbid; but mature. Probability charts rate death at 100 percent. Preparing for it is as sensible in the physical aspect as in the spiritual. Being realistic, a colleague and I devoted a lunch hour to explore the local situation. We engaged the amiable salesman of the memorial park in conversation about his real estate. Without intending to belittle the seriousness of such an involvement, our experience was hilarious.

"Now here is our new mausoleum, set here in the quietude of these old live oaks. . . ." We walked into the dignified stone building and he drew our attention to the burial spaces.

"We recommend that you purchase two locations, side by side, as husband and wife. We want to assure you that the partition in this case is removed, so that you can be together. . . ." Together! Very prospective! But *here?!*

"The spaces are air-conditioned, with very comfortable distribution of fresh ventilation constantly. . . ." Was that somehow to alleviate the discomfort of dying in a Texas summer?

The climax came later, however,

when we decided to secure a plot in the park for the eventuality. Once more the salesman extolled the virtues of the property, the surroundings, the view (We really needed that!), the shaded and well-drained property, and the perpetual care. It was clearly designed for the living, not the dead. I thought of the words of Hebrews 11: "They looked for a city . . ." not a cemetery!

Having conducted scores of funerals, I have walked through enough neatly manicured memorial lawns to know that we only have a thin slice of time on planet earth. It is not enough just to live out our allotted time, even though well-prepared for eternity. We need to recall Moses' words of the ninetieth psalm: "Teach us to number our days aright, that we may gain a heart of wisdom." The Hebrew word for wisdom means the skill of living one's life well. What impact am I making for the Lord with people? It has to be made right now. ◆

Last Rights

here's a tiny piece of real estate in Texas with my name on it. I bought it; I did not really want to. I never go to look at it; I don't even like to think about it.

Dad would have been nearly fifty-eight years old that raw October day when I sat beside his open grave with my mother and sisters. I felt I could not cry another tear, yet I could not stop. The man who had been my early confidante, my childhood companion, my sturdy dependable father, was gone—down there in that hole.

Texas sunshine finally thawed my soul; family responsibilities forced me to move back into the stream of life. But one fact remained central: It *can* happen in my family—and it has. Death does not always strike "over there."

Family consultations followed; at least we should make preliminary plans.

"OK, we'll do it right," we concluded. "We're young, healthy, but realistic. Contact the funeral home; ask for information."

"Mr. Hendricks, you are extremely wise. You and your wife are to be commended for your foresight, your wisdom, your attention to the necessary. . . ."

"Yes sir, we understand. When may we see the property?"

Few customers, I am sure, come to see grave sites with detachment such as mine. Like a reluctant toddler reciting lines in assembly, I came to the park and I wouldn't let myself take it too seriously.

"Imagine me," I thought. "Riding around a memorial park in the back of this slick black limousine, looking at burial lots!" It was incongruous with my life which bubbled with babies and school books, shopping lists and house guests.

The names of the sections were mellifluous: Cool Waters, Garden of the Gentle Shepherd, Rainbow Glen. Tranquility reigned. The salesman who drove kept up a steady patter of sales talk.

"Now that we've seen a goodly selection, we should ask the Missus. . . ." He turned his coiffured gray head and flashed his institutional smile.

"It doesn't really matter too much," I shrugged. "You see, we'll probably never ever use it."

His eyes stared hard at me.

"I mean, I think Christ is coming back to take us first."

"Ahem—ah—yes, well. . . ." He cleared his throat. "But you *do* want to buy one?"

"Oh, yes." What I wanted was to get out of there. Cemeteries have never been my favorite place to linger.

To date the burial plot is still unused. I continue to hope that the money was spent totally in vain, that our Savior will return for us before we ever need an earthly grave. Death never gets an invitation from me. I hate him even in fairy stories. I see him in fantasy dancing around peeking in people's windows, always trying to get inside. Yet he is no fairy tale character; God said he is the last enemy to be destroyed. God also said he has been de-fanged: "Where, O death, is your sting?" We may have to meet him, but he is unarmed.

Nevertheless, whether our Lord allows us to die and be buried in that plot, or whether He catches us away, still living, He will come for us. What a glorious prospect: "If I go . . . I will come back and take you to be with me that you also may be where I am." (John 14:3) ◆

Conclusion: Flashbacks of Faith

ow faith is being sure of what we hope for and certain of what we do not see. . . . And without faith it is impossible to please God, because anyone who comes to him must believe that he exists and that he rewards those who earnestly seek him. (Hebrews 11:1, 6)

For Howard and Jeanne Hendricks, realities of the human race have been gushing past us for more than half a century, often at floodtide. These pages have dipped into our private runoff barrel to sample for our readers life as we have known it. A question rises: What motivates you two? Where are you coming from?

Hidden in the heights of the New Testament is a sparkling stream where God's most esteemed servants are registered. A gallant crew mans the oars of Hebrews 11; each person in this account walked in the pages of the Bible with a force that erupted in this gilt-edged roll call. Abraham, Noah, Joshua, and a host of others—giants of faith. From these greats we observe that faith grows not through isolation but through involvement. Abraham pitched his tent in a wilderness populated with idolaters; Noah

constructed his ark in a dry land of scoffers of God;
Joshua mobilized his troops against insuperable odds
of heathen hordes.

In imitation, we have walked not in
the hallowed halls of academia or ecclesiastical
shrines; mostly we have jogged along with the rank
and file of common folk, letting them see up close
we are merely clay pots—ordinary, but marked for
the Master's use. We believe that God is interested
not only in branding us as His servants, but in
refining, polishing, and maturing us. He not only
imparts faith; He develops it. Our motivation for
living is capsulized in the prayer of Moses: "Teach
us to number our days aright, that we may gain a
heart of wisdom." (Psalm 90:12) ◆